ESSAYS TO HELP YOU WRITE

EXAMPLES TO HELP IMPROVE YOUR ESSAY WRITING SKILLS

HARSHIT KUMAR

Contents

CHAPTER ONE

NEWSPAPERS

<u>Introduction</u>

The newspaper is the most authentic and reliable source of information as it only prints the news after proper investigation. Newspapers are delivered to our doorstep early in the morning. We can read the news by having a cup of tea and get to know what is going on around the world. Newspapers are economical as we get information at a very low cost. They are easily available and are also printed in different languages. Thus, newspapers make it easier for people to read news in their native language.

Newspapers cover different columns, and each column is reserved for a particular topic. The employment column provides information related to jobs. This column is very useful for youth who are searching for suitable jobs. Similarly, there are other columns such as the matrimonial column for finding the perfect match for marriages, a political column for news related to politics, a sports column for analysis and opinion on sports updates, etc. Other than this, there are editorials, readers, and critics' reviews that provide a wide variety of information.

The first newspaper to be printed in India was called Gazette Bengal. It was published by an Englishman, James Augustus Hicky in 1780. This newspaper was followed by the publication of other newspapers like Indian Gazette, Calcutta Gazette, Madras Gazette Courier and Bombay Herald in the coming years. After the first freedom struggle of 1857, the number of newspapers appearing in different languages of India continued to grow. At the time of this freedom struggle, media expansion in India was not large. However, after India became independent, the expansion of newspapers continued.

A newspaper is an important prerequisite for democracy. It helps in the proper functioning of government bodies by making citizens informed about government work. Newspapers act as powerful public opinion changers. In the absence of a newspaper, we cannot have a true picture of our surroundings. It makes us realise that we are living in a dynamic world of knowledge and learning. Daily reading of the newspaper will help improve English grammar and vocabulary, which is especially helpful for students. It also improves reading skills along with learning skills. Thus, it enhances our knowledge and broadens our vision.

Newspapers contain advertisements which are essential to run a paper. So, along with news, newspapers are also a medium of advertising. Advertisements related to goods, services and recruitment are broadcast. There are also missing, lost-found, and government-release ads. Though these advertisements are useful most of the time, sometimes they result in misleading people. Many big companies and firms also advertise through newspapers to enhance their brand value in the market.

There are numerous advantages of the newspaper, but on the other side, there are some drawbacks too. Newspapers are a source of exchanging diverse views. So, they can mould the opinion of people in positive and negative ways. Biased articles can cause riots, hatred and disunity. Sometimes immoral advertisements and vulgar pictures printed in the newspaper can severely damage society's moral values.

Deletion of the vulgar ads and controversial articles removes the above-mentioned demerits of the newspaper to a great extent. Thus, an active reader cannot be misled and deceived by journalism.

CHAPTER TWO

EDUCATION

Education, for the most part, is simply a set of skills and ideas that we are meant to take in, absorb, and implement into our lives. They range from knowledge about how to balance a checkbook to understanding Hegelian philosophy. Without learning these skills and ideas, it's impossible for us to grow as people. We need education in order for us to be the best version of ourselves – not only educated but thoughtful beings who have learned how life works by living it themselves. There's no way around it; education is one of the most important things in life and touches just about every aspect of our being – emotionally, intellectually, and otherwise. Without it, we are incapable of growing and thriving as human beings; with it, we stand a chance.

What is the purpose of school? A school is a place where you go every day from 5th grade until the year after high school graduation. Then you go to college. The purpose of school is so that we can learn how to become productive members of society and better people so that we can become happier in life. Not just for us but also for our countries and communities. We need a good education because it teaches us the skills that will help us do great things in life and not waste our time on bad things such as drugs, alcohol, etc.

Education is necessary for us to grow in every aspect of our lives, but that doesn't mean that every subject a school teaches is worth learning. The difference between high school and college isn't the subjects we learn – both schools teach us things like history, math, English, and science – but how we learn them. In high school, teachers simply throw information at us to memorize for tests; as if the only thing that matters in life is getting good grades with little effort and regurgitating knowledge on command.

What's the purpose of high school? In high school, we learn about many things like history and sciences, which help us become better people because we will be able to know many different events that happened in history. Also, we are able to understand how far people have come in things like science, mathematics, and English. We also learn good morals such as not lying to other people or doing certain actions that can hurt other people or damage their lives. Lastly, high school is a gateway to college or jobs.

Once we enter college, though, things are different. College students are no longer forced to memorize facts, but rather are given the opportunity to learn subjects intellectually; it's not about us regurgitating what we know but rather actually learning and analyzing. Northwestern University defines college as "the level of education where students actively learn, think, talk, write, challenge ideas, work with others and introduce new knowledge." Forcing us to memorize what we learned in high school is the antithesis of learning; teaching is essential for us to develop our minds. College teaches us skills in order to become a better person, which is vital for our self-development, and without them, we are incomplete.

One of the most important things colleges teaches is how to think critically and analytically. This is a skill that has no true substitute – one that allows us to step back from the world we live in and analyze it logically so we can make decisions as adults rather than simply go through life without them. Without this skill, we're simply people who know how to do things but aren't truly able to make independent decisions because they don't know the full issues involved behind the decisions they've made. Critical thinking skills allow us to be able to differentiate between different sources of information and understand that no single source can be considered completely unbiased. Dr. Lawrence Kohlberg, a cognitive psychologist, says "there are many kinds of intelligence: emotional intelligence, street smarts, practical intelligence... We need to understand that any single definition [of intelligence] is too narrow." Dr.

Howard Gardner also supports this claim with his multiple intelligences theory; he asserts (and has proven) that there are many kinds of intelligence and there is no singular way for people to be intelligent. Instead, there are many different ways for a person to learn and be intelligent. Gardner's theory is one of the most important theories in the field of psychology because it reframes intelligence as more than just knowledge or skill and allows us to think about intelligence in a way that we haven't before.

Education is very important. However, what is the true meaning of education? Education is something we learn in our childhood. It is not just a school or college education but also something that touches every part of our life.

What are some of the great benefits of education? Well, first of all, it teaches us important skills like math and science. These are important for us to learn because they help us do everyday things, like balancing checkbooks and going to work. They also teach us how to become good citizens through knowledge about history and politics. College teaches us how to make good decisions by educating us in economics. These are all skills that we would like to learn.

What is the importance of education? Well, I mean...it's important for us to have a good education to be able to do many things and be able to do harder things like understanding something instead of just knowing it or something that is complicated and difficult. It's important for us to learn and develop our knowledge about something that will help us think about it differently, something that will help us understand it better, know many things about it, and have the ability to remember what we learned so we can use what we learned in our daily life. Education helps people become more intelligent and improve their value system. Education helps us become more knowledgeable and improve our minds. Education helps us understand and improve our lives. Education is important because it helps us learn more about ourselves, our community, our society, and the world around us.

Educating ourselves is the best thing we can do to help change the world around us. We need to help educate children because when they grow up and become adults they are better people. They will be able to understand the needs of their community and become educated so that they are not ignorant and can change the world in ways that benefit all of society. We need a good education because it helps us understand our goals and dreams as well as our mistakes in life because we know what we should be doing so that's why it's important for us to study hard. If we don't have a good education, than we will have a lot of problems with growing up, understanding ourselves, becoming successful on our own, etc. Also, we need to be educated so that we can learn the difference between good and bad and know what to do in life. Education helps us understand what we should be doing because it teaches us important things in our life that we will be able to tell about later when we want to talk about our mistakes. Also, it helps us stop wasting our time on bad things that can damage our lives and cause us pain and suffering.

Education is important for everyone, it's the key to a better life, and learning is fun. If we have a good education in our life that's great for us. We will know what to do in life and be prepared for what we are going to encounter. We will also be able to enjoy our lives more than if we didn't get any education our whole life. Education is the key to success in life, we should do everything possible to get an education because it's very important for us and it's very helpful.

CHAPTER THREE

WILDLIFE - A WARNING TOPIC

Like forests, wildlife consisting of animals, birds, insects, etc. living in the forest is a national resource, which not only helps in maintaining the ecological balance but is also beneficial for various economic activities that generate revenue from tourism. The rich flora and fauna also play a major role in maintaining the ecological balance of a region. There was a time when human needs were minimal and there was bare interference in the wildlife. There is no denying the fact that due to urbanization, pollution, and human interventions wildlife is rapidly disappearing from the planet.

Today the biodiversity of the world is threatened due to the extinction of species. There are thirty-five hotspots around the world, which supports 43% of birds, mammals, reptiles, and amphibians as endemic. The IUCN has compiled a list of species and has classified the different species under extinct, critically endangered, less endangered, vulnerable, near threatened, and least concerned. This list is called the Red Data Book. According to the World Wildlife Fund (WWF), the number of birds, animals, marine and freshwater creatures has dropped by almost one-third of its earlier population.

One of the major reasons for the constant decline of wildlife is human's ever-increasing demands and greed that have led to deforestation and habitat destruction. For development and urbanization, man has chopped down trees to build dams, highways, and towns and this has forced the animals to retreat further and further into the receding forests.

Rapid industrialization and urbanization due to the fast growth in population in recent decades have taken a heavy toll on wildlife. Global warming and extensive environmental pollution have largely threatened wildlife as they lead to habitat destruction and rising temperature.

There is a huge demand for animal fur, skin, meat, bone, etc. across the globe that has led to a decrease in the wildlife population. Poachers kill the animals for the illegal trading of their body parts. For example, elephants are massively poached for ivory, rhinoceros are poached in Assam for their horns. The desire to keep animals in captivity or their desire to consume certain animals as exotic food has resulted in the disappearance of many animal species such as tigers and deer.

Forest fires, food shortage, increase in the number of predators, extreme weather conditions and other extraneous reasons have led to the extinction and endangerment of many species. For instance, the recent forest fires in the Amazon (Brazil), Uttarakhand (India), Australia, etc. lead to the death of many animals every year.

Many types of animals, birds, and fauna are needed to retain the ecological balance. They are considered necessary for scientific research and experiments that will benefit mankind. Let's learn how to conserve wildlife.

The protection and conservation of wildlife is the need of the hour. Some conservation efforts which are widely implemented are given below:

First and most importantly, humans need to have control over their needs. We need to prevent man from felling trees unnecessarily. Trees should be replanted if they are felled.

Pollution is one of the major causes that have led to the destruction of the habitat of animal species. Pollution of the environment like air pollution, water pollution, and soil pollution hurts the entire ecosystem. It has become of utmost importance to control environmental pollution.

More campaigns must be launched to raise awareness in humans on the need to keep our environment clean. A man should be responsible to maintain a healthy and balanced ecosystem so they should be cordial with the environment. More organizations like PETA should be set up to create awareness among people for the protection of wildlife.

The man should consciously put a check on the rapid growth of the population. The slow growth of population will decrease the rate of urbanization and that will have a major impact on the preservation of wildlife.

Wildlife sanctuaries should be made to ensure the protection of the areas of ecological significance. Under the Wildlife Protection Act, 1972 various provisions for protecting habitats of wildlife are made by constructing national parks and sanctuaries. These parks and sanctuaries ensure the protection and maintenance of endangered species.

Illegal activities like hunting, poaching, and killing animals, birds, etc. for collections and illegal trade of hides, skins, nails, teeth, horns, feathers, etc. should be strictly prohibited and severe punishments and fines should be imposed on people who do these kinds of activities.

Communities come together to take various conservation initiatives such as the establishment of community forests, raising their voice against illegal activities, creating awareness among the masses, raising voice for the rights of the animals, conserving animals of cultural significance, and many more. For example, members of the Bishnoi community of Rajasthan are very vocal against poaching activities in the region.

Many countries have taken the initiative to help animals by proclaiming various birds and animals either as national animals or as protected species. In India, the government has launched a program of Joint Forest Management to protect the wildlife and their habitat. Under this program, responsibilities have been assigned to the village communities to protect and manage nearby forests and the wildlife in them. Animal species have the right to live just like humans. Therefore, we should take every step to conserve them and ensure their survival and betterment.

Wildlife is an integral part of our planet. Wildlife plays a significant role in the ecology and the food chain. Disturbing their numbers or in extreme cases, extinction can have wide-ranging effects on ecology and humankind. Valuing and conserving forests and wildlife enhance the relation between man and nature. We want our future generation to be able to hear the lions roar and peacocks dancing with their extravagant feathers and not just see them in picture books. We must take steps today or else it will be too late and we should always remember

"Earth provides enough to satisfy every man's needs, but not every man's greed."

-Mahatma Gandhi

CHAPTER FOUR

HEALTH IS WEALTH

Health is God's gift to us. Health refers to the physical and mental state of a human being. To stay healthy is not an option but a necessity to live a happy life. The basic laws of good health are related to the food we eat, the amount of physical exercise we do, our cleanliness, rest, and relaxation. A healthy person is normally more confident, self-assured, sociable, and energetic. A healthy person views things calmly, and without prejudice.

"The Dalai Lama, when asked what surprised him most about humanity, answered "Man! Because he sacrifices his health to make money. Then he sacrifices money to recuperate his health. And then he is so anxious about the future that he does not enjoy the present; the result being that he does not live in the present or the future; he lives as if he is never going to die, and then dies having never really lived." This signifies that individuals don't prioritise their mental health to earn money. Some even work 24 hours a day or seven days a week.

However, you have the option to remain balanced. So, balance work and fitness daily. Always strive to keep a cheerful as well as a concentrated routine. It is necessary to plan ahead of time. In any case, one must maintain a good mental, bodily, and emotional state, and no professional or counsellor can assist you unless you desire to live. The will to live in the moment and make the most of it awakens the ideal strength within you, and you are the only one who can never let yourself fall apart.

We live in a super-fast age. The Internet has shrunk the world dramatically and people are connected 24x7. Multitasking is the order of the day, as we struggle to fulfill our responsibilities for everyone in life. In this fight, we often forget to spare time for ourselves. The stress levels continue to build up until one day a major collapse may make us realize that in all this hectic activity, we have forgotten to take care of one important thing – our health.

As we spend days shuttling between hospital and home, putting our body through one test after another, trying to find out what has gone wrong, we are forced to remember that 'Health is indeed Wealth'.

In earlier days, life was very simple. People worked for a stipulated time, often walked everywhere, ate more homemade food, did household chores, and enjoyed a healthy balance in life.

Now people have cars and bikes to commute, so they walk less. With the demand for more working hours, people are awake till late at night and indulge in more junk food than home-cooked food. Modern equipment at home has reduced the labour work and increased dependency on this equipment. People don't have enough time to exercise or even get enough sunlight. Nowadays people are living very unhealthy lifestyles.

Unhealthy living conditions have increased the contraction of people to various diseases like obesity, diabetes, heart attacks, hypertension, etc. This has alarming implications in the near future. So it is very important to focus on our health as much as we focus on our work. Moderation in food habits, daily exercise, and balanced work-life can surely make a big difference to our health and body. When a person stays mentally and physically fit, his actions and decisions are more practical and logical and hence he is more successful in life. Furthermore, good health has a direct impact on our personality.

It's crucial to consider how much self-control you have to keep a healthy lifestyle. Research reveals that changing one's behaviour and daily patterns are quite tough. According to the data, whether a person has a habit of smoking, drinking alcohol, doing drugs, or any other substance, it is extremely difficult to quit. A study found that 80% of smokers who tried to quit failed, with only 46% succeeding.

A healthy body has all the major components that help in the proper functioning of the body. The essential component is the state of physical health. Your life term extends when you maintain good physical fitness. If you are committed to exercising with a sensible diet, then you can develop a sense of well-being and can even prevent yourself from chronic illness, disability, and premature death.

Along with physical fitness, a good mental state is also essential for good health. Mental health means the emotional and psychological state of an individual. The best way to maintain good mental health is by staying positive and meditating.

However, unlike a machine, the body needs rest at regular intervals. A minimum of six to seven hours of sleep is necessary for the body to function optimally. Drinking plenty of water and a balanced diet is also very important for your body. If you violate the basic laws of good health, like working late hours, ignoring physical exercise, eating junk food, it will lead to various ailments like hypertension, heart attacks, and other deadly diseases.

Every year on April 7th, World Health Day is celebrated. The World Health Organization (WHO) hosted the inaugural World Health Day on April 7, 1950, to draw the entire world's attention to global health.

Every year, the World Health Organization (WHO) comes up with a new theme for public awareness, such as "Support Nurses and Midwives" in 2020. This supports the situation of COVID-19, where healthcare workers are saving lives day and night without worrying about their health.

The WHO also operates a global health promotion initiative to align equality so that individuals can take control of their lives, "every life matters," and consider their fitness. The government promotes numerous health policies, including food security, workplace quality, and health literacy, in schools, colleges, workplaces, and various community activities.

Children need to maintain good physical and mental health. With an increase in the pressure of studies and over-indulgence in modern gadgets, children are losing the most precious thing, which is health. These days, they barely play in the playgrounds, they are more inclined towards junk food and spend more time on the screen. These unhealthy activities are slowly sabotaging their health. Parents should concentrate on the physical and mental health of their children, and inculcate good habits for maintaining a healthy lifestyle from a tender age.

Cleanliness also has a major role to play in maintaining good health. Taking a bath every day, washing hands before eating meals, brushing twice a day, changing clothes regularly, etc. are important habits to maintain good health.

Society is witnessing gloomy faces as a result of children and their parents' excessive usage of a computer, mobile phone, and the Internet. They are constantly using these technological items, oblivious to the fact that they may harm their health. Teenagers are frequently discovered engrossed in their electronic devices, resulting in mishaps.

The usage of electronic devices frequently results in anxiety and hostility. Excessive usage of these products has been linked to cancer, vision loss, weight gain, and insomnia.

Emotional development is another crucial component that should not be disregarded because it determines whether or not a person is healthy. An emotionally healthy person should have a solid sense of logic, realisation, and a realistic outlook.

Health is Wealth because if we are not healthy then all our wealth, fame and power can bring no enjoyment. Keeping fit and healthy is indeed not an option but a necessity.

CHAPTER FIVE

ISRO – Indian Space Research Organisation

ISRO, the Indian Space Research Organization, is India's national space agency that is located in the city of Bengaluru. Furthermore, the Department of Space Government of India controls the ISRO space agency. Let us learn more about this space agency with this essay on ISRO.

The formation of ISRO took place in the year 1969. Furthermore, the vision behind the establishment of ISRO was to develop and harness space technology in national development. Moreover, this development and harnessing of space technology were to take place while pursuing space science research and planetary exploration.

ISRO is the successor of the Indian National Committee for Space Research whose establishment took place in the year 1962. ISRO now enjoys the reputation of being among the elite space agencies in the world.

As of now, ISRO is the primary Indian agency to perform activities related to the development of new technologies, space exploration, and space-based applications. Moreover, ISRO is among the only six government agencies that operate large fleets of artificial satellites, deploys cryogenic engines, undertakes extraterrestrial missions, and has full launch capabilities.

Throughout many years, ISRO incorporates space service for the benefit of the common man as well as the nation. Moreover, the maintenance of one of the largest fleets of communication satellites and remote sensing satellites takes place by ISRO. They serve the roles of fast and reliable communication as well as Earth observation.

The first Indian satellite that was built by ISRO was Aryabhata, whose launching took place on April 19th, 1975. Furthermore, 1980 was another important year for ISRO because the launching of the Rohini satellite took place. Moreover, the successful placing of Rohini in the orbit took place by SLV-3.

In the year 2014 January, ISRO made use of an indigenously built cryogenic engine for GSLV-D5. Also, this was the launch of the GSAT-14 satellite. Most noteworthy, this made India one of the only six countries to develop a cryogenic technology.

Apart from technological capabilities, a lot of contribution has taken place by ISRO in the field of science. Furthermore, ISRO is in charge of its own Lunar and interplanetary missions. Moreover, ISRO controls various specific projects for the promotion of science education, and also to provide data to the scientific community.

The development of two rockets has taken place by ISRO, which are the Polar Satellite Launch Vehicle (PSLV), and the Geosynchronous Satellite Launch Vehicle (GSLV). Moreover, ISRO sent Chandrayaan-1, a lunar orbiter, on October 22nd 2008, which made the spectacular discovery of lunar water in ice form.

The Mars Orbiter Mission was sent by ISRO on November 5th 2013, which made its entry into the orbit of Mars on September 24th 2014, thereby making India successful with its attempt to Mars.

There is no doubt that ISRO is really the pride of India. Furthermore, it has boosted the reputation of India in the world as a nation of scientific thought and development. Hopefully, ISRO will continue on its noble mission of space and technological exploration in the future.

CHAPTER SIX

INTERNET

We live in the age of the internet. Also, it has become an important part of our life that we can't live without it. Besides, the internet is an invention of high-end science and modern technology. Apart from that, we are connected to internet 24×7. Also, we can send big and small messages and information faster than ever. In this essay on the Internet, we are going to discuss various things related to the internet.

It is very difficult to estimate the area that the internet cover. Also, every second million people remain connected to it with any problem or issue. Apart from that, just like all the things the internet also has some good and bad effect on the life of people. So the first thing which we have to do is learn about the good and bad effect of the internet.

Good effects of the internet mean all those things that the internet make possible. Also, these things make our life easier and safer.

Bad effects of the internet mean all those things that we can no longer do because of the internet. Also, these things cause trouble for oneself and others too.

You can access in any corner of the world. Also, it is very easy to use and manage. In today's world, we cannot imagine our life without it.

From the time it first came into existence until now the internet has completed a long journey. Also, during this journey, the internet has adopted many things and became more user-friendly and interactive. Besides, every big and small things are available on internet and article or material that you require can be obtainable from internet.

Tim Berners-Lee can be called one of the main father of internet as he invented/discovered the WWW (World Wide Web) which is used on every website. Also, there are millions of pages and website on the internet that it will take you years to go through all of them.

The Internet can be used to do different things like you can learn, teach, research, write, share, receive, e-mail, explore, and surf the internet.

Because of internet, our lives have become more convenient as compared to the times when we don't have internet. Earlier, we have to stand in queues to send mails (letters), for withdrawing or depositing money, to book tickets, etc. but after the dawn of the internet, all these things become quite easy. Also, we do not have to waste our precious time standing in queues.

Also, the internet has contributed a lot to the environment as much of the offices (government and private), school and colleges have become digital that saves countless paper.

Although, there is no doubt that the internet had made our life easier and convenient but we can't leave the fact that it has caused many bigger problems in the past. And with the speed, we are becoming addict to it a day in will come when it will become our basic necessity.

CHAPTER SEVEN

DIGITAL INDIA

The "Digital India" campaign was launched by the government of India to uplift the usage of technology in India. The objective was to make Government services easily available to the citizens electronically by improving its online infrastructure all over the country. The process would be structured to increase internet connectivity to make the country digitally empowered. It helps to reach out to the masses and encourages them to use technology in their daily lives. Prime Minister Mr. Narendra Modi launched the campaign on July 1, 2015. The initiative aims at connecting rural India with the help of high-speed internet connectivity.

To be able to deploy various digital services across the country, it is necessary to create a strong digital infrastructure, especially in rural areas of the country. The interior regions of the country either have very little or mostly do not have any electronic network. This is the reason behind establishing a digital network across the country. Bharat Broadband Network Limited, the governmental body that is responsible for the execution of the National Optical Fiber Network project is responsible for the Digital India project as well. Bharat Net aims to connect 2,50,500 gram panchayats across the country to a high-speed internet network via an optical fiber network. 4,00,000 internet points will be established all across the country as part of the program, from which anybody will be able to access the internet.

A major component of the Digital India campaign is to deliver government services and other essential services digitally. It is easier to change the way of delivering services from physical to digital. Many services of the Government of India were digitized under the Digital India Campaign.

All ministries would be linked under this scheme, and all departments will be able to reach out to the people with fundamental services like health care, banking, education, scholarships, gas cylinders, water and electricity bills, and judicial services. The daily monetary transactions of people were also converted into digital mode. To ensure transparency in the transactions and curb corruption all the money transactions are being made online, and are supported by one-time passwords.

For full participation of the people of India, the competency that they need to have is called Digital Literacy. The basic behavior, knowledge, and skills required to effectively use digital devices are mandatory. Desktop PCs, laptops, tablets, and smartphones are the digital devices used for the purpose of communicating, expressing, collaborating, and advocating. The mission of Digital Literacy will be covering over six crore rural households.

With the Digital India Programme, the Government of India is hoping to achieve all-around growth on multiple fronts collectively. The objective of the Government is to target the nine 'Pillars of Digital India' that are identified as Broadband Highways , Universal Access to Mobile Connectivity , Public Interest Access Programme , E-Governance , E-Kranti , Global Information , Electronics Manufacturing , Training in Information Technology for Jobs , Early Harvest Programmes , To directly benefit the citizens of all future government schemes.

The awareness of the importance of technology has been successfully created among the masses of India by the Digital India campaign. There has been a vast growth in the usage of the internet and technology in the past few years. The Panchkula district in Haryana was awarded the best and top performing district under the Digital India campaign on the 28th of December 2015.

So far, services such as digital lockers, my government website, e-education, scholarships, pensions, ration cards, PAN cards, Aadhar cards, e-insurance, and e-health have been made accessible under this plan. The goal has been established for the Digital India project to be completely implemented by 2019.

Technology giants from all over the world paid attention to the Digital India campaign and are readily and happily supporting the initiative. Even Mark Zuckerberg, the CEO of Facebook, had changed his profile picture to support Digital India. He started a trend on Facebook and promised to get the WiFi Hotspots in rural India working. Google started on its commitment to providing broadband connectivity at 500 railway stations in India. Microsoft agreed on providing broadband connectivity to 5,00,000 villages in the country. Microsoft is also making India its cloud hub via the Indian data centers. Oracle planned on investing in 20 states to work on Smart City initiatives and payments.

A digitally connected India is aimed at the growth of the social and economic status of the masses in the country. The development of non-agricultural economic activities could pave the path for such an achievement, for providing access to financial services, health, and education. Information and Communication Technology alone cannot directly impact the overall development of a country. Basic digital infrastructure could help achieve overall development.

Literacy and regulatory business environments also could help achieve the same. It will be a very profitable approach because it relieves the burden of spending time on paperwork and allows people to dedicate their time to other aspects of government. It is extremely efficient and beneficial for government employees who operate on a big scale.

CHAPTER EIGHT

ARTIFICIAL INTELLIGENCE IN OUR LIVES

Artificial Intelligence is the science and engineering of making intelligent machines, especially intelligent computer programs. It is concerned with getting computers to do tasks that would normally require human intelligence. AI systems are basically software systems (or controllers for robots) that use techniques such as machine learning and deep learning to solve problems in particular domains without hard coding all possibilities (i.e. algorithmic steps) in software. Due to this, AI started showing promising solutions for industry and businesses as well as our daily lives.

Importance and Advantages of Artificial Intelligence

Advances in computing and digital technologies have a direct influence on our lives, businesses and social life. This has influenced our daily routines, such as using mobile devices and active involvement on social media. AI systems are the most influential digital technologies. With AI systems, businesses are able to handle large data sets and provide speedy essential input to operations. Moreover, businesses are able to adapt to constant changes and are becoming more flexible.

By introducing Artificial Intelligence systems into devices, new business processes are opting for the automated process. A new paradigm emerges as a result of such intelligent automation, which now dictates not only how businesses operate but also who does the job. Many manufacturing sites can now operate fully automated with robots and without any human workers. Artificial Intelligence now brings unheard and unexpected innovations to the business world that many organizations will need to integrate to remain competitive and move further to lead the competitors.

Artificial Intelligence shapes our lives and social interactions through technological advancement. There are many AI applications which are specifically developed for providing better services to individuals, such as mobile phones, electronic gadgets, social media platforms etc. We are delegating our activities through intelligent applications, such as personal assistants, intelligent wearable devices and other applications. AI systems that operate household apparatus help us at home with cooking or cleaning.

Future Scope of Artificial Intelligence

In the future, intelligent machines will replace or enhance human capabilities in many areas. Artificial intelligence is becoming a popular field in computer science as it has enhanced humans. Application areas of artificial intelligence are having a huge impact on various fields of life to solve complex problems in various areas such as education, engineering, business, medicine, weather forecasting etc. Many labourers' work can be done by a single machine. But Artificial Intelligence has another aspect: it can be dangerous for us. If we become completely dependent on machines, then it can ruin our life. We will not be able to do any work by ourselves and get lazy. Another disadvantage is that it cannot give a human-like feeling. So machines should be used only where they are actually required.

CHAPTER NINE

Technology

The word technology comes from the two Greek words, 'techne' and 'logos'. Techne means art, skills, or craft, and Logos means a word, saying, or expression that expresses inward thought. Thus, technology means the skill to convey an idea to reach a goal. But nowadays, the term technology mainly signifies the knowledge of tools, machines, techniques, crafts, systems, and organisation methods to solve a problem. Today, technological advancement has provided the human race with the ability to control and adapt to their natural environment.

How Has Technology Changed Our Lives?

Various innovations and development took place in the field of technology which has made a significant impact on our lives in different ways. With the invention of technology, we become more powerful. We have the ability to transform the environment, extend our lifetime, create big and interconnected societies and even explore various new things about the universe. Today, we use technology from morning to evening, from the simplest nail cutter to television and personal laptop. Technology has touched all aspects of our lives, whether it is mobile phones, kettles, kitchen microwaves, electric cookers, television, water heaters, remote control, fridge, and other larger communication systems such as internet facilities, railways, air routes, and so on. Thus, technology plays an extremely crucial role in the lives of human beings.

Advantages of Technology

The advancement in technology has made our lives easier, more comfortable and enjoyable. It has reduced the effort and time required to complete a task, thus enhancing the quality and efficiency of work. Technology has become a part of our life and benefited us in many ways. Today, we can communicate with people living in any city or country. Communication has become much faster and easier as we are just a click away from people. In education, technology has played a vital role, especially during the COVID-19 breakdown period. It has brought virtual and online classes for students and teachers across the globe to share knowledge, ideas and resources online. Moreover, technology has made it easier for students to understand complex concepts with the help of virtualisation, graphics, 3D animation and diagrams.

Technology is considered to be the driving force behind improvements in the medical and healthcare field. Modern machines have helped doctors to perform operations successfully. Due to technology, the lifespan of the common person has increased. There are many more sectors, such as banking, automation, automobile, and various industries, where technology is making significant changes and helping us.

Disadvantages of Technology

Although we have so many advantages of technology, there are also disadvantages. Robots and machines have taken over the job of many people. Instead of bringing people together, technology has made them socially isolated. People now spend most of their time on smartphones or computers rather than interacting with other people. Technology in education has reduced the intellectual and analytical ability of students. It is like spoon-feeding to students as they don't have the reasoning and aptitude skills to think differently. Technology has raised the issue of internet privacy. So, one has to be very careful while using banking passwords to make online transactions.

Future of Technology

The future of technology seems to be exciting but also scary. Futuristic predictions in technology can dish out some exciting or scary visions for the future of machines and science. Technology will either enhance or replace the products and activities that are near and dear to us. The answer to our technological dilemma about what will be the upcoming technological innovation in the future is not surprising. In the past, technology was mainly focused on retaining more information and efficient processing, but in the future, it will be based on industrial robots, artificial intelligence, machine learning, etc.

Conclusion

Technology alone cannot help in building a better world. The collateral collaboration of machines and human effort is required for the progress and prosperity of the nation. We need to develop a more robust management system for the efficient functioning of technology.

CHAPTER TEN

Sustainable Development

Sustainable development is a central concept. It is a way of understanding the world and a method for solving global problems. The world population continues to rise rapidly. This increasing population needs basic essential things for their survival such as food, safe water, health care and shelter. This is where the concept of sustainable development comes into play. Sustainable development means meeting the needs of people without compromising the ability of future generations.

What Does Sustainable Development Means?

The term "Sustainable Development" is defined as the development that meets the needs of the present generation without excessive use or abuse of natural resources so that they can be preserved for the next generation. There are three aims of sustainable development; first, the "Economic" which will help to attain balanced growth, second, the "Environment", to preserve the ecosystem, and third, "Society" which will guarantee equal access to resources to all human beings. The key principle of sustainable development is the integration of environmental, social, and economic concerns into all aspects of decision-making.

Need for Sustainable Development?

There are several challenges that need attention in the arena of economic development and environmental depletion. Hence the idea of sustainable development is essential to address these issues. The need for sustainable development arises to curb or prevent environmental degradation. It will check the overexploitation and wastage of natural resources. It will help in finding alternative sources to regenerate renewable energy resources. It ensures a safer human life and a safer future for the next generation.

The COVID-19 pandemic has underscored the need to keep sustainable development at the very core of any development strategy. The pandemic has challenged the health infrastructure, adversely impacted livelihoods and exacerbated the inequality in the food and nutritional availability in the country. The immediate impact of the COVID-19 pandemic enabled the country to focus on sustainable development. In these difficult times, several reform measures have been taken by the Government. The State Governments also responded with several measures to support those affected by the pandemic through various initiatives and reliefs to fight against this pandemic.

How to Practise Sustainable Development?

The concept of sustainable development was born to address the growing and changing environmental challenges that our planet is facing. In order to do this, awareness must be spread among the people with the help of many campaigns and social activities. People can adopt a sustainable lifestyle by taking care of a few things such as switching off the lights when not in use; thus, they save electricity. People must use public transport as it will reduce greenhouse gas emissions and air pollution. They should save water and not waste food. They build a habit of using eco-friendly products. They should minimise waste generation by adapting to the principle of the 4 R's which stands for refuse, reduce, reuse and recycle.

The concept of sustainable development must be included in the education system so that students get aware of it and start practising a sustainable lifestyle. With the help of empowered youth and local communities, many educational institutions should be opened to educate people about sustainable development. Thus, adapting to a sustainable lifestyle will help to save our Earth for future generations. Moreover, the Government of India has taken a number of initiatives on both mitigation and adaptation strategies with an emphasis on clean and efficient energy systems; resilient urban infrastructure; water conservation & preservation; safe, smart & sustainable green transportation networks; planned afforestation etc. The Government has also supported various sectors such as agriculture, forestry, coastal and low-lying systems and disaster management.

www.ingramcontent.com/pod-product-compliance
Lightning Source LLC
Chambersburg PA
CBHW060524120726
48002CB00011B/3308